# 21st Century Skills Library

## CITIZENS AND THEIR GOVERNMENTS

# GOVERNMENT AT WORK

*Tamra Orr*

Cherry Lake Publishing
Ann Arbor, Michigan

CHERRY
LAKE
Publishing

Published in the United States of America by Cherry Lake Publishing
Ann Arbor, MI
www.cherrylakepublishing.com

Photo Credits: Page 15, Photo Courtesy NASA

Library of Congress Cataloging-in-Publication Data
Orr, Tamra.
   Government at work / Tamra Orr.
      p. cm.—(Citizens and their governments)
   ISBN-13: 978-1-60279-059-9
   ISBN-10: 1-60279-059-0
   1.  United States—Politics and government—Juvenile literature.  I. Title.
II. Series.
   JK40.O77 2008
   320.973--dc22                                    2007006760

*Cherry Lake Publishing would like to acknowledge the work of*
*The Partnership for 21st Century Skills.*
*Please visit* www.21stcenturyskills.org *for more information.*

# TABLE OF CONTENTS

# CHAPTER ONE

## TAKING GOVERNMENT FOR GRANTED

*The local fire department is one of the most obvious ways that people can see their tax dollars at work.*

P eople often take many parts of government for granted. If they need

help, they dial 911, and the police or firefighters are on the way. If they need to go somewhere, they know they can hop on a

bus, jump on the subway, or use the highways. When

they retire, they know the government will provide

health insurance. If they turn on the tap, they expect

fresh, clean water to come out.

It is easy to take these things for granted because

they seem to have always been there. They are just

part of daily life. This was not always true, however.

Most have developed over time as people have

needed them. The funds for most of these services

come from taxes and fees. But where do the various

governments get the funds? From you, of course!

What things in your life do you take for granted that actually come from the government? Think carefully, so you don't overlook any of them. Choose a couple and think what life would be like without them.

## How Much to Put that Out?

The city of Rome in modern-day Italy was once the center of a huge empire. In about 79 B.C., a man named Marcus Licinus Crassus had a very clever idea. He knew that there was a need in Rome for some kind of fire protection, and he knew he was the one who could provide it. He built a horse-drawn water tank and waited for a fire.

Crassus was not just being kind, however. He was a businessman, and he saw a moneymaking opportunity. He would ride along with his men to the scene of a fire and before they started to put out the flames, Crassus would negotiate the price for

*Crassus is said to have had as many as 500 people working in the "fire brigade" that helped make him so wealthy.*

the service with the landowner. Often he asked for the property itself as

payment. Then the owner would have to pay Crassus rent—for life! As a

result, Crassus became one of Rome's richest landlords.

## 21st Century Content

Some small towns, today and in the past, have volunteer firefighters. These are usually people in the town who feel it is part of their responsibility as good citizens to help others. In some other countries, however, the government and its people are too poor to pay firefighters, and the people have to "make do" with whoever shows up to help when a fire breaks out. In these cases, neighbors help neighbors.

Fortunately, today no one in America has to pay firefighters before they start extinguishing the flames.

Firefighting is one of many public services that government is responsible for. This includes hiring, paying, and training the firefighters. It includes building and maintaining firehouses. It includes buying fire hoses and fire trucks—and replacing them when they are worn out. It includes paying medical bills for the firefighters and retirement benefits, too.

# CHAPTER TWO

# FEDERAL TAXES AND PROGRAMS

Benjamin Franklin said, "In this world, nothing is certain but death and taxes." Many people agree. Taxes are something everyone pays. The right to collect taxes is in the Constitution. Article 1, Section 8 says, "Congress shall

*Some federal tax revenue is used to maintain and protect the White House and pay the salaries of the White House staff.*

have power to lay and collect taxes, duties, imposts and excises, and to pay the debts and provide for the common defense and general welfare of the United States."

Taxes are the number one way that the federal government raises money. The biggest source of all is the **income tax** each person pays on money made over the year. This money is sent to the Internal Revenue Service (IRS), a bureau of the United States Treasury Department. In 2003, the IRS took in almost $2 trillion! That is about $6,300 per person. Usually, the federal income tax is due to the government on April 15 of every year.

*Federal tax money funds the U.S. Army, Navy, Marines, Air Force, and Coast Guard.*

One of the most important duties of the federal government is to provide the national defense, and a great deal of federal tax money goes to this aim. This money pays for equipment such as guns, ships, tanks, and airplanes. It pays for soldiers' uniforms, training, meals, and beds. It also pays for the military academies at West Point, Annapolis, and

Colorado Springs. Since the terrorist attacks in 2001, the amount of money used for national defense has increased dramatically.

Federal taxes pay for some important services that people rarely see but definitely need. One of these is the Centers for Disease Control and Prevention (CDC). This group studies new diseases such as bird flu and looks for ways to make them less dangerous.

Another important government agency is the Department of the Treasury. It is responsible for printing money—and finding **counterfeiters,** too! Federal taxes also pay the salaries of the president, members of Congress and the Supreme Court.

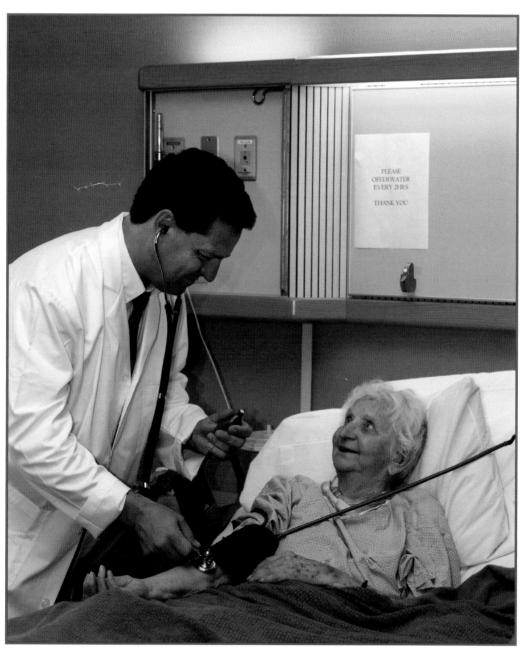

*Every year, the hospital stays of millions of older Americans are largely paid for through the Medicare program.*

Federal taxes also pay for Medicare and Medicaid programs. Medicare is a health insurance program for citizens age 65 and over. It pays for items such as doctor visits, hospital stays, X-rays, and other tests. In 2006, the program served more than 41 million Americans and cost more than $277 billion.

Medicaid is a health insurance program for citizens younger than 65 who have low incomes and few resources. Many of the people served by Medicaid are children.

*Between 1968 and 1972, NASA used federal tax dollars
to send Apollo missions to the moon.*

Federal taxes also pay for things that it would be difficult or even

impossible for small groups or individuals to do. One of these is space

exploration. The National Aeronautics and Space Administration (NASA)

was formed in 1958. In 1969, it was NASA that landed Americans on

the moon. NASA is now planning a return to the moon as well as more

projects to Mars and beyond.

Space exploration is so expensive that few nations have even attempted it. In fact, the U.S., Russia, Canada, and others have worked together on the Space Shuttle and International Space Station.

The federal government also manages places we all like to go—parks! These include big and famous parks such as the Grand Canyon,

*In 2006, park staff at Grand Canyon National Park handled 1,540 medical emergencies and search and rescue missions.*

Yellowstone, and the Everglades. The National Park

Service (NPS) also oversees parts of American history

such as the Statue of Liberty and Mount Rushmore.

In addition, the NPS maintains some unusual spots

such as inventor Thomas Edison's laboratory in

New Jersey, Abe Lincoln's home in Illinois, and

nineteenth century factories in Lowell, Massachusetts.

Since the federal government is charged with

representing the United States to the rest of the

world, federal tax money pays for **embassies** around

the world. In fact, the United States has embassies in

more than 150 countries. In some countries, there are

offices in several cities. For example, there are offices

### 21st Century Content

Some other nations do not have the financial resources and people to have embassies in almost every country around the globe. Some countries also don't feel it is necessary to have embassies everywhere. In addition, bad relations may cause countries to close their embassies in some countries. The United States closed its embassy in Iran after revolutionaries took it over in 1979 and held more than 60 U.S. citizens captive for more than a year.

**Learning & Innovation Skills**

One of the newest parts of the federal government is the Department of Homeland Security. It was created after the terrorist attacks in 2001. What kinds of responsibilities do you think people in this department might have?

in ten cities in Mexico! The Department of State also issues **passports** to U.S. citizens and provides **visas** to people who want to visit here.

The federal government is responsible for many areas of American life. It oversees special hospitals for military **veterans**. It protects important national documents such as the first versions of the U.S. Constitution. Once every decade, it must count every single person in the nation. It runs the Central Intelligence Agency and the Federal Bureau of Investigation to catch "bad guys." It even makes maps, from ones that show where people live to others that indicate natural resources and hazardous waste sites.

# CHAPTER THREE

# STATE AND LOCAL GOVERNMENT

*Plowing the streets is a major responsibility of cities
and towns across the country every winter.*

When many people think about government, they envision the White

House or perhaps a battleship. The federal government does play a large

**21st Century Content**

One tax that the United States does *not* have is the Value Added Tax (VAT). However, it is widely used around the world in countries such as Mexico, Russia, Sweden, Japan, Israel, Chile, Iceland, South Korea, South Africa, and the United Kingdom. This tax is built into the selling price of an item, and it is usually collected from the maker or seller, not the buyer.

role in most Americans' lives. However, local and state governments often have as much—if not more—impact on a people's daily existence.

States and cities get some of their financing from the federal government. However, other sources of funding are needed, so many states use a state income tax. States often use a **sales tax,** too. This tax is a small percentage of the cost of an item and is added to most purchases, large or small, made in the state. However, many states do not tax key items such as groceries or medicine.

*Property taxes may increase if the owner paves a driveway, renovates a business space, or makes other improvements.*

Two-thirds of the money to support most cities comes from a **property tax**. This tax is based on the value of the land and buildings in a specific place. This tax applies to homes, businesses, farms, and almost every place else. However, hospitals, schools, and churches are usually **exempt**. The tax

## 21st Century Content

License plates not only generate money for states, they also are extremely useful to police officers when trying to identify a specific vehicle. License plates are also widely used around the world. However, the exact size and shape may be different from those in America. For example, Namibia, England, and Australia use license plates that are much longer and narrower than American ones.

is collected yearly, like income taxes are. An **assessor** studies each property and determines its value. A percentage of this value becomes the amount of the property tax.

Cities and states have other ways of raising funds. One of these is license plates for cars and trucks. Usually, the owner has to purchase the metal plates initially and then also buy annual stickers after that. Some cities require special stickers, too. Sometimes, such special fees are used for specific projects. The funds from license plates, for example, may be directed to pay for road maintenance or police activities.

*Most states require that residents purchase licenses for cars, boats, motorcycles, SUVs, buses, trucks, and other vehicles.*

# CHAPTER FOUR

# COMMUNITY SERVICES

*Building schools is expensive! For example, Indiana districts spent
more than $365 million for new elementary schools in 2005.*

Now that states and communities have collected their taxes, just

where does all this money go? The single largest expense for most can be

summed up in one word: schools. From kindergarten through high school,

*Police protection is a key duty of all communities and can cost more than $1 billion a year in big cities such as Chicago.*

schools need teachers, books, desks, computers, basketballs, test tubes,

maps, electric lights, lunchrooms, gyms, heat, clean hallways, libraries, and

dozens of other items. It all adds up fast.

For most communities, the second largest expense is for police and fire

protection. Most citizens hope to never need a police officer or firefighter.

However, these two groups need to be available on a moment's notice all

day, every day. That often means communities must employ several "shifts" of police officers and firefighters. Equipment can be a major expense, too.

Think of police cars and fire trucks, which must not only be purchased

but also maintained.

## From Faucets to Flushing

Other major community costs are for **sewage** and **sanitation**. In fact,

these two are usually a community's third largest expense. Clean water

*The wastewater treatment plants in Honolulu, Hawaii,*
*treat more than 40 billion gallons of water yearly.*

is something that Americans expect to find every time they turn on a faucet, and they also expect that wastewater will disappear quickly and efficiently. Raw sewage can be lethal, especially if it reaches the drinking water supply. Many cities have extensive sewage treatment plants to ensure that doesn't happen.

## Time for Fun!

Many communities also provide entertainment for their citizens. Think of that neighborhood park or the town swimming pool. The swing set and tetherball get used in the summertime, while the ice rink gets a workout in January. The band shell

Think about the fun places to go and things to do in your community. Are there any activities you wish were available?

## 21st Century Content

Building and maintaining public transportation systems is an important task for cities around the world. For example, London, Moscow, Paris, Toronto, Bangkok, and Barcelona all have extensive subway systems, as well as many public bus routes.

provides a place for the high school orchestra to play as well as a spot for local politicians to address voters. The baseball diamond gets a lot of use by the Little League teams.

## Getting Around

For large cities, public transportation can be an essential service. New York, Washington, and Chicago have extensive subway and bus services. Seattle even has a **monorail**. Hundreds of thousands of Americans travel to and from work on these low-cost systems every day. They can move many people at one time but create less pollution and use less energy than individual cars. Commuters like the systems because they can read the morning paper while somebody else watches the road!

## Other Community Offerings

Most communities also have libraries with books, videos, and magazines to check out. However, the library may also provide meeting rooms for local clubs and special classes. If people want to study their genealogy, they may be able to take a class about it at the library.

Some towns also have "community centers" where citizens can take classes in yoga and square dancing, for example. The center may also offer low-cost courses in knitting, painting, and other hobbies.

**21st Century Content**

Very large cities like New York have zoos and museums! Toronto has several city museums celebrating different eras in the city's history. Wellington, New Zealand, has a city zoo, as does St. Petersburg, Russia.

# Glossary

**assessor (uh-SES-er)** official who evaluates property for tax purposes

**counterfeiters (KOUN-ter-fit-erz)** people who make fake money and other goods such as paintings

**embassies (EM-buh-seez)** buildings for offices of diplomatic officials

**exempt (ig-ZEMPT)** free from an obligation or duty to which others are subject

**income tax (IN-kuhm taks)** annual tax paid on the money earned that year

**monorail (MON-uh-reyl)** transportation system on a single rail that is typically elevated

**passports (PAS-pohrts)** official government documents that certify identity and citizenship and permit travel abroad

**property tax (PROP-er-tee taks)** annual tax on the value of land and buildings at a specific place

**sales tax (seylz taks)** city or state tax that is added to the cost of purchases at the time of sale

**sanitation (san-i-TEY-shuhn)** application of measures designed to protect public health, especially in relation to sewage

**sewage (SOO-ij)** water-carried wastes from toilets, sinks, bathtubs, etc.

**veterans (VET-er-uhnz)** people who have served in the armed forces

**visas (VEE-zuhz)** official authorization to enter and travel within a particular country

# FOR MORE INFORMATION

## Books

De Capua, Sarah. *Paying Taxes*. New York: Children's Press, 2002.

Grote, JoAnn. *The Internal Revenue Service: Your Government and How It Works*. Philadelphia: Chelsea House, 2001.

Kishel, Ann-Marie. *Government Services*. Minneapolis: Lerner Publications, 2006.

Reeves, Diane L. *Career Ideas for Teens in Government and Public Service*. New York: Facts on File, 2005.

## Other Media

To find out more about the federal government, go to
*http://www.whitehouse.gov/kids/*

Learn more about NASA at
*http://www.nasa.gov/about/highlights/what_does_nasa_do.html*

Search out national parks and monuments in your own state at
*http://www.cr.nps.gov/*

# INDEX

## ABOUT THE AUTHOR

**Tamra Orr** is a full-time writer and author living in the gorgeous Pacific Northwest. She loves her job because she learns more about the world every single day and then turns that information into pop quizzes for her patient and tolerant children (ages 16, 13, and 10). She has written more than 80 nonfiction books for people of all ages, so she never runs out of material and is sure she'd be a champion on *Jeopardy!*